Shattered – A Journey Through the Pieces

Rodney Damon Collins

This book is dedicated to the memory of Beatrice Jackson

To my Super Def Homegirl and Granny, although my heart is heavy, eyes are filled with tears, my mind is filled with joy and laughter. No more suffering, no more pain but you are full of joy because you get to spend eternity with other loved ones once again. How do you say so long, farewell, or goodbye? I'll miss you, and I will meet you at the final destination one day.

"The Gift of Life"

Your heart was bigger than anyone could imagine

You were the light that shined through the dark

The rock who became the mountain

A seed that blossomed into a beautiful flower

The vessel that gave life to many

The rain to nurture your family

You were the pillar to hold the foundation together

You had a sense of humor to keep the world laughing

And a smile to light up a room

Most of all, as the Mrs., you would tell it like it is, if

somebody

didn't want the answer, they should not ask the

question

You didn't sugarcoat anything

Yet, you were such a giving and

loving person who loved others unconditionally

Forever my Super Def Homegirl

-Sharmaine Martin

Table of Contents

"Dreams"

Hold Fast to Dreams

For if dreams die

Life is a broken-winged bird

That cannot fly.

Hold fast to dreams

For when dreams go

Life is a barren field

Frozen with snow.

- Langston Hughes

Introduction

"My broken brilliance will shine a light in the darkness." – Matt Hardy

As a child, I remember standing in front of my mirror and picturing myself as a very successful person. As I studied myself and imagined how tall I would be in the future, I dreamed of what I could be in the near future. What I didn't realize is that at some point in my life there would be brokenness. That mirror which represented my dreams would also be shattered. The good news is that each of the shattered pieces of my dreams would be put back together to form an incredible masterpiece.

We are all searching for purpose. Each person on this planet has a dream. There is a legacy that we all want to leave. Through this journey we call life, there will be times when we experience a shattered dream. Through each broken piece comes growth. Each piece comes together to create a beautiful portrait of our lives and to show the path we were intended to walk. *I want you to know that you're not alone.* Although various forms of adversity or different forms of disappointment may have broken our spirits, we must discover how we can use those moments to better our lives. *Do I have all the answers? No. Is this an answer to all your questions? No.* This book is meant to be an encouragement for those of you who are looking for purpose and are trying to find it in material possessions, a successful career or personal relationships.

It has been said that the average human lives 28,000 days. This equates to 76.71 years, 40,320,000 minutes, 672,000 hours. While this time may seem like a lot of time, there's another important fact associated with the 28,000 days. The average human sleeps 1/3 of this time. In essence twenty-five years of our life is spent sleeping. As a result, we spend fifty years living. My question for you to ponder as you read this book is what have you done with your time lately, and what will you do with the minutes, hours, and days you have left?

If I am honest with myself, I have times when I've wondered why am I here? In other words, why was I born? Is life about growing up, going to school, raising a family, retiring, and then dying? I've struggled with the issue of purpose in my pursuit of living my best life. Life for me has always been a roller coaster ride. I mean I've played the game as I was coached. In most instances, our families, schoolteachers, mentors, ministers, and politicians have taught us how to play the game and succeed through their words, actions, and beliefs. Oftentimes, their words of advice were for us to do well in school, be good citizens and obtain a great paying job. Some even stated you should never become part of a profession that does not provide a stable income; in other words, you should steer clear of jobs related to the arts. In their minds singing, painting and acting are hobbies – not occupations or vocations. *Were we coached correctly?* Well, I did the required work and earned a diploma from high school. Then I graduated from college, worked a good corporate job, yet I was still unfulfilled. If we are completely honest with ourselves, everyone on earth is searching for his or her purpose. I am no different than anyone else. In my journey, I've experienced numerous heartbreaks. These disappointments have led me to experience shattered dreams. However, I've learned not be defeated. As we take away life lessons from the shattered pieces, we must be warriors who are willing to pick up even the smallest pieces of the broken dreams and begin to rebuild and construct bigger and better dreams! Truthfully, the struggle gives us the strength to endure and to triumph over the shattered pieces in our journey.

No matter what age you are, you still matter, there's still purpose, and there's still a need to have hope about your future. What I've discovered in my life is that there are many suggested ways to define success and purpose according to people and their plans for you, but God has the best plan. There are a variety of key principles that I've learned through my journey that have helped me to define my life's purpose and to determine what truly matters. As you read this book, think about your passions, your purpose, and your journey. How do they line up with God's divine plan for your life?

Remember that God created you and knows

your deepest desires.

Chapter 1
Suddenly

**""Life is not measured by how many
breaths we take, but how many moments
that take our breath away."**

Suddenly, I felt a jarring hit! I hit my

head on the ground and blacked out. I woke

up in an ambulance with my mom and dad

draped over me and two air casts on my

legs. I had been hit by a drunk driver and

had no idea what was going on. I recall that

when I blacked out, it was as if I were still

conscious of what was happening around

me. It was so bright. For a moment, it

seemed as if I was looking at my body from the outside. I didn't hear a voice calling me, but I did feel as though I was rushing towards something. At only 12 years old, I began to see how quickly things change in a person's life. One minute I was riding my bike and having a good time; the next minute I was seconds away from death. I couldn't recall everything that happened to me, but one thing for sure, I didn't want to die. There were things I wanted to do. In other words, I did not believe it was my time to leave earth because I had not fulfilled my life's purpose.

One of the biggest misconceptions about following God and finding our purpose is that events in our life should have a smoother path. In the past, I've been told that when something wasn't working, that it wasn't meant for me. In my walk with God, I've discovered that while God is there to protect and guide us, following Him is one of the most challenging things that we can do. It requires faith to believe that life will work out. There's an incredible journey that God has planned for His creations and children. Yet, this life is brief. Why live it in hiding just waiting for eternity? I invite you to live dangerously and see how full your life will be. What does it mean to live dangerously? It means being willing to step into unfamiliar territory. Everyone is not called to sacrifice their lives on a battlefield, but there are things in life that each and every one of us is called to live out. Will you throw in the towel when things get tough or you cannot see what God's next move is going to be? I challenge you to be sensitive to that quiet inner voice that speaks to you. Live your truth today! There's a life that we all want: a life of freedom and a life of purpose based on our gifts and talents.

We want to matter. If you look at the different social media sites, you will see evidence of people's seeking validation from others and people's enjoying recognition for their own accomplishments. Also, the need for recognition can first be seen when we are children and are excited to show our parents our accomplishments – no matter how minor the tasks. Children are ecstatic to receive affirmation and validation. Oftentimes, parents can be instruments in helping their children to discover their passion in life. What do your children love and enjoy? In what fields or subjects do your children excel?

As I reflect back over my life, I discovered my life's passion when I was a young child because I dreamed often without setting limitations on myself. We've all had that time in school when the teacher would ask you what do you want to be when you grow up? Well, I remember hearing that question and wondering what does that mean? As a 5th grader, I couldn't really answer that question because I was more focused on what we were having for lunch that day rather than what I would be doing 20 years from then. There were things that I liked to do. I had dreams, but I wasn't ready to define them. I loved watching television and reading books. One of my favorite television shows was *Knight*

Rider. I loved watching KIT, the high-tech car, along with Michael Knight's weekly adventures. Also, reading books has always been a passion and escape for me. I recall playing with my toys and creating entire plots, including commercials, while playing with them. I believe this was a time in my life that my dreams were trying to make themselves known to me.

Each person on this planet is here for a very specific purpose. If we are all honest with ourselves, most of us want to live a life of purpose. What does it mean to live a life of purpose? We must all realize that we matter and that in some way our lives can make an impact on others. It's a desire within each and every one of us to live a fulfilled life, and each one of us can live our best life by flourishing in a field that best uses our natural gifts and talents. Many are looking for acceptance when they first walk into a church, a classroom, and even a store. They want to be greeted by someone and be acknowledged. This desire is rooted in our longing for validation. However, we get true validation and fulfillment when we live a life of purpose by doing something we love and value.

Chapter 1 - Reflection Questions

1. What did you enjoy as a child? Why?

2. When you were a child, what did you dream of becoming as an adult?

3. What are your natural gifts and talents?

4. How can you use your gifts and talents impact people's lives in a meaningful way?

5. If you did not have any limitations or obstacles, what

would you choose to do for a

career? Why?

Chapter 2
Me, Myself, and Why?

**"Dreams are illustrations...from
the book your soul is writing about you"**
-Marsha Norman

Around the age of 17, I shared some of
my dreams with my parents.   I recall
asking them about these dreams and what
could they mean.   One dream in particular
would have me speaking in front of large
crowds.   Their response was that only God
could help me to understand what the dream
meant.   It wasn't an encouragement to me
because I wanted an answer.   You could say
that I was impatient.   I didn't understand that
my impatience at the time was rooted in not

understanding that when God gives you a dream, that dream is for you and no one else. Therefore, my parents couldn't fully comprehend what I was trying to communicate to them. I didn't fully understand it at the time. I had a great childhood, and I have two wonderful parents. I'm thankful to have them today, but this should be a lesson for parents everywhere. When your child comes to you with certain desires or dreams, understand that it's not your role to tell them what it means. As a parent, I've learned that even if I cannot tell my son and daughter what their dreams mean, I can help them unpack it. A

23

very important skill that every parent should develop is the ability to pay attention to his or her child. When a child shows excitement about something, help him or her to learn more about the subject.

When I was a senior in high school, there was a competition called "Super Fella." The top five guys in the senior class based on popularity were nominated to compete for the title of "Super Fella." We were each tasked with coming up with a way to promote ourselves. This was my first experience as a writer, producer, and director. I decided to write a sketch based on the *Arsenio Hall Show*. A part of the competition involved each candidate's giving a speech to the student body. My first major speech was as a senior in high school in front of nearly 2,000 people. It was an amazing feeling. I was comfortable. Yes, I was cool, calm, and collected. I enjoyed having influence. It felt as though I really mattered! That's when I discovered a key element of purpose. *We want to matter!* Let me pause here for a second and ask you, where do you matter? At what point in your life did you feel that you really mattered to someone or something? What were you doing? That could've been the beginning of something great in your life.

25

Dreaming about my future is something that I always did. My best friends and I loved sports. Every Saturday, we would gather with friends at an open field and play football from sun up to sun down. In the winter, we would often shovel our driveways in order to play basketball. We believed that our skills and love of sports would provide a job for us in the future. When I would watch television, I would see athletes living successful lives. At least in my eyes that's what their lives appeared to be. Their homes were mansions: five or six bedrooms minimum, swimming pool, hot tub, large front and back yard, surrounded by a gate. *I wanted that life.* Anytime I picked up a basketball or football, I believed that I was getting closer to my goal of being wealthy. In essence, what I thought that I wanted was the American Dream. In my desire and pursuit of my dreams, I didn't realize the cost that would be associated with becoming successful.

What is the cost of being successful? I've taken a look at the lives of many people who have achieved success and although their paths are different, the type of sacrifices are similar. Tyrese Gibson, a gifted actor and singer, once said, "The dream is free. The hustle is sold separately."

I can sit and stare at the sky and dream about what I want my life to be, but eventually I have to get up and put in the work to see it come to pass. Someone may ask how does this look? For me, it means being satisfied with walking by myself. I have my family at my side, but my life is no longer filled with a large number of people. As I have seen people in my life leave, I had to understand that there was a focus that my dreams require. *My challenge to each person is that you be willing to not be in the crowd in order to focus and prepare for what you desire to happen in your life.* Kobe Bryant, one of the greatest basketball players ever, had an incredible focus. Kobe

28

is just one example of someone being willing to sacrifice something in his present situation to position himself for future greatness. While in high school, he would go to the gym at 5:00 A.M. before school and practice. In the afternoon, he would practice until 7:00 P.M.! During this time, he sacrificed going out with friends. He was on a mission.

Chapter 2 - Reflection Questions

1. What does it mean for you to matter?

2. Do you have a dream that keeps you up at night?

3. What sacrifices are you willing to accept in pursuit of your dream?

Chapter 3
Temporary Disappointments
Are Not Permanent Endings

**"We must accept finite
disappointment, but never lose infinite
hope."
-Martin Luther King, Jr.**

A disappointment is temporary. When I
was twelve years old, I played for a baseball
team. It was my first experience in
organized baseball, and I loved it. It gave
me an opportunity to build relationships
with people whom I might not have met in
my neighborhood. We were good; I mean
really good. We were preparing to play the
semi-final game to decide which team would
play in the championship. After dominating
our league, we went in cocky and arrogant.

31

Just like most people who forget what it takes to achieve and maintain success, we were beat. As a team, we took it very hard. There was a lot of disappointment. We were crying and even cursing. It was a shattering moment. On a Sunday morning, a couple days after the game, my baseball coach called my home. He told my parents that one of my teammates had committed suicide. I mean he was only twelve years old! What would bring a boy to the point of giving up hope in life, putting a gun to his head and ending it all? This was my first experience with how a crushed dream can lead someone to take extreme methods. How could someone make a permanent decision to end a temporary problem? I had so many questions, and I didn't know how to handle my teammate's suicide. This event in my life should have been processed. There was the question of why did he do it? Where did he do it? Did he feel alone? There wasn't much of an explanation as to why my friend did this. I was afraid and struggling. I can honestly say this was my first experience with how dangerous a momentary disappointment can lead someone to make a permanent decision.

When I was younger, I had a dream to win the NFL Super Bowl and to be on the cover of a major magazine. My making it to the NFL would put me in a position to financially take care of my entire family and to create opportunities for those who really needed help. I recall scoring touchdowns and even seeing myself one day winning a close game with an incredible run. *Picture this,* our team is down by 6 points with a less than 15 seconds remaining. We're on our own 35-yard line. I run up to the line of scrimmage. The defender lines up on the other side of the line. The quarterback calls out the signals, "Hut 1! Red 23!" The ball is snapped to the quarterback. I start running straight for about 10 yards. Then I make one move to the left, then to the right and the ball is released. As I'm running down the field, I turn my head and raise my hands to catch the ball. It lands in my hands, and then I began to sprint down the field right between two defenders. Within a matter of seconds, I burst into the end zone and the game is over! Well, that dream didn't happen. In the summer before my senior year in high school, I attended a football recruitment camp at the University of Michigan. I met a recruiter for Bowling Green State University. He let me know that there was some interest in my skills from what he had seen that week. I was very excited. After the camp, I returned home to continue football workouts. I was excited about the preparations for my senior season! Also, I received a letter from the Bowling Green recruiter. He let me know of Bowling Green's interest in me and that I would be invited up to school to take a look at the football program. One day while at practice, we were conducting some drills. One of the drills involved my diving on a loose football. As I dove on top of the ball, I felt a pop in my shoulder and an immediate sharp pain followed. I had dislocated my shoulder; this was an intensely painful injury. My shoulder had swollen up. My uniform had to be cut off and before I knew it. My parents were with me as the doctor was preparing to put my shoulder back in place. A few weeks later, I was told that I would need to miss my senior season due to the injury. The trainer on our team didn't want me to risk further injury. As a result, I was no longer considered a college football recruit. This was a major disappointment to me. Because of this crushing experience, my anger and frustration were probably the most intense that it had ever been. It was the first time I had to come to the realization that the dream of a N.F.L. career was most likely going to die.

A wise person once told me that, "Often times your dreams are a strong indication of how God has wired you. Do not ignore them." What this meant to me is that there are unique desires that God has given me. It serves as a compass for my life. One thing that I've always known is that I have dreams that connected to my purpose. For example, I have been given a deep desire to see people encouraged and living life to their fullest potential. Something that breaks my heart is to see someone who isn't living up to his or her fullest potential. As I mentioned previously, this life is brief. The time that we have must count for something.

38

If we don't live to make an impact in someone's life that drives him or her towards his or her purpose, we are merely taking up space. As a result, we begin to discover our purpose and see our dreams fulfilled through having an attitude of humility and genuine concern for the well-being of our fellow man.

Chapter 3 - Reflection Questions

1. What was your first painful disappointment?

2. How did you handle this disappointment?

Chapter 4
The Carefree College Years?

**"The biggest adventure you can
take is to live the life of your dreams."
-Oprah Winfrey**

Being a first-generation college student
was an incredible achievement for my
family and me. Neither one of my parents
had the opportunity to attend college. Going
to college meant that I was venturing into
unknown territory for my family and myself.
While there was a sense of excitement, there
was also a heavy weight associated with this
experience. I felt a burden to make sure that
I was the one to graduate from college.
While I know that it was important to my

parents for me to graduate from college, I added to this pressure with my own thoughts. My parents never told me that it would disappoint them if I didn't graduate from college. I created this burden in my head. The thought would cross my mind, "If I don't graduate from college, then I will fail my family." As a result, I started my college education with an unnecessary self-inflicted burden. What I began to see was that the biggest obstacle to my progression is the person that I would see in the mirror every day. *In other words, my toughest enemy was my inner me.*

When you first enter college, there are many opportunities presented. There are ways to engage socially, educationally, culturally, and financially. One of the worst mistakes that I ever made was filling out an application for my first credit card. For me this meant that I was getting ready to receive my first sign of independence, my own credit card. What a horrible mistake! When I first received the credit card, I went directly to the store. Why? Because who doesn't want to feel as though he or she can get his/her own. The crazy thing is that I thought I was really being an adult. You know, having the ability to get what you want when you want it. Or so I thought that's what it was. In reality, I was spending tomorrow's prosperity - today. The credit card had a limit of $1,000, definitely not a responsibility that should be given to an 18-year-old college student. It didn't take long for that $1,000 limit to be exhausted. The feeling was great until about thirty days later I received my first credit card bill. I slowly opened the bill and to my surprise my limit had been reached! I thought to myself, what is this? I actually had the nerve to get mad at the credit card company. My first major financial lesson. I learned that buying things on credit can cost you. The items that I purchased on that card were worth nothing by the time that I paid the debt off. Once again, I used the credit to buy something that I couldn't afford and had to use future income to resolve a past debt. What I learned is that this was more a lesson in patience then finances. Using credit cards without the money to pay the bill lead to unnecessary stress and debt. Being impatient is a self-inflicted injury. In my life, impatience has been one of the main reasons for my personal struggles.

My college experience was enjoyable, but it was also very stressful. It was supposed to be an exciting time. I mean you're away from home. I remember checking into my room that was centrally located on campus. Then there is the memory of hanging out in the student union while checking out the college women! This was finally my chance to experience what life would be like living on my own without all of the financial concern and responsibility associated with moving out of the house. I really wanted to succeed in college. My first semester of college seemed to be off to an incredible start. I made the Dean's list my very first semester. Also, I was preparing to go through the Resident Advisor process. Becoming a

Resident Advisor was a big deal for me because it would help me financially and professionally. Then it was time to go home for winter break. Soon after my arrival home, I was hit with a reality. My parents were sacrificing so much to send me to school. What I mean by that is that Christmas didn't look like it used to. I saw the past due bills that my parents didn't think I saw. I witnessed a struggle, a sacrifice; there was a price that someone was paying for me to experience this next phase of life. It was at this point that my heart began to break for my parents. They had given so much! I wanted to do whatever it took to achieve success for both my family and myself. I'm forever grateful for an incredible sacrifice. Mom and Dad, I appreciate you and all that you did for me to become the man that I am today! I have the ultimate example of sacrifice right in front of me.

As I was approaching my junior year in college, I was still struggling with what path was meant for me. However, I met the woman who would walk this adventure of life with me, Falanda Jackson. She was visiting the college for the weekend with a friend, Erinn Speed. I was in a fashion show, the "Jabberwock". Put on by the women of Delta Sigma Theta, the "Jabberwock" was a time when the "who's who" on campus would show off their talents on stage. *Well, not to toot my own horn, but I was looking really good.* I later learned that Falanda noticed me. She couldn't keep her eyes off me! As I walked across the stage, Falanda was inquiring about me. Erinn replied, "Oh, that's just Rodney." Falanda told me later that she thought that I did not have the greatest reputation on campus. She decided not to show any further interest in me.

The following year, Falanda was in a play on campus, and I recall watching her. I didn't know her yet, but I did tell one of my friends, "Watch, before we leave college, she will be mine." I knew that I wanted to meet her, but I heard that she was in a relationship with someone, so I left her alone. One year later, unbeknownst to me, Falanda was staying in the same residence hall as I was. I saw her a couple times but didn't approach her. There were a few reasons why I didn't introduce myself. First, I assumed that she was still in a relationship. Second, I had decided to just focus on graduating from college. Third, I was

49

scared! Later, I learned that Falanda was watching me! As she watched me, she thought to herself, that's the guy! After we met and developed a relationship, she shared this story with me. I guess she didn't want me to think that she was some kind of stalker.

One evening, I was preparing to attend a party on campus. My friend Louis Farmer, one of the most comical people whom I have ever met, called me. He said, "Don't go anywhere, I got someone for you to meet!" I really wasn't interested in meeting anyone. I had been through a few disappointing relationships. My focus was on other things: graduating from college, figuring how I was going to make a living, and finding out who I was becoming. Nevertheless, I agreed to wait for Louis to come by my room. Well, I must say that I'm glad that I waited because when I opened the door, I saw the girl, my girl – Falanda Jackson! She was the one! It was that feeling of the crush that you have as a child. It was that excitement of meeting someone that you really wanted to meet. She was the one! I had to stay cool. She was the girl that I said would be mine before graduating from college. I turned and tried to hide my excitement and politely greeted

51

her. Everything in me wanted to run up and ask her "Do you know how long I've been waiting for you!" After that, we developed a relationship. We didn't make it official right away, but we might as well have because we spent time together each day. Meeting Falanda was a significant part of my journey. One of the biggest challenges that I had was that I wanted someone who could go on the journey with me. I wanted to meet this person before I achieved a level of success in my career. Throughout my life, I've seen many people achieve a certain level of success, but they don't have someone with whom to share it. I've always believed what is the purpose of being successful if you don't have someone to share the experience with. Yes, Falanda is a very important part of my life and my journey.

Chapter 4 - Reflection Questions

1. Who is your "ride or die" (someone who is walking with you) while you are on your journey?

2. How has a self-inflicted injury impacted your life?

Chapter 5
Is This What I Signed Up For?

**"Trust in dreams, for in them is
hidden the gate to eternity."**
-Khalil Gibran

It was an incredible feeling to graduate
from college. I was entering the adult
world, and I thought I was gaining complete
independence. I grew up in Toledo, Ohio,
but my first employment opportunity after
graduation from Bowling Green was in
Cleveland, Ohio. The cities are only two
hours apart, but for someone who was
preparing to embark on an incredible new
journey, this might as well have been
moving across the country. As I was

moving from my hometown to a new city, I recall driving to my new home and having an incredibly sinking feeling. My summer vacations were gone! I mean, during my years in college, there was a sense of freedom. Freedom to sleep in instead of going to class, freedom to stay up late and hang out with friends, freedom to leave the lights on in your room without worry about increasing the light bill. There were freedoms, freedoms, and more freedoms. The freedoms that I had grown so accustomed to enjoying would be gone soon.

I was happy to receive a great opportunity to work in Corporate America. This included the company car, a salary, benefits and travel. While I had this great opportunity, there was also a part of me that wasn't sure about the job. Was there a different path that I should be taking? There were other options, but I was so focused on finally making some money that I didn't give those other options much attention. I said to myself, "It's time to get paid. Aren't you tired of being a broke college student?" The unsettled feelings in myself were telling me that I should really evaluate the job. *Is this what I really want?* I didn't listen to that inner voice. For what other reason do you go to college but to get a good job offer and a great start at life? Right? Other options were offered and available. I had an opportunity to pursue an advanced degree for free through my university. I thought about pursuing an advanced degree in the field of my choice, while working as a Hall Director. In addition, law school was on the table for me. If you watched enough episodes of *LA Law,* it made the profession look glamorous. I dreamed about being an attorney. I even took time to shadow a mentor in the field of law to learn more. There was also something that was in my heart that I would never share with people. I knew that I had a gift. I could act, and I really enjoyed it. I recall as a kid one of my friends calling me the world's greatest pretender. While he was trying to be funny, he was actually affirming a gift that I had. I thought about pursuing the acting, but I was very concerned about the thoughts of people. So concerned, that I tabled that desire and went on to pursue more practical options. This tug felt as though I couldn't breathe when I thought about it. I would become anxious. Also, I felt a strong tug on my heart to look into a seminary. When the thought would come, I would immediately throw it out of my mind because I had no desire to go to graduate school. I was tired of being broke. In addition, I couldn't see the role a seminary degree would play in my corporate career.

Accepting a position in Corporate America seemed like the right thing to do. There were some important events going on in my life. Did I mention I was preparing to marry the love of my life? This was one of the main influences on my decision to accept a job in Corporate America. I knew that I couldn't get married without having a way to provide for my wife. Besides, I recall Gwen Guthrie's song that said, "Ain't nothing going on but the rent, you got to have a j.o.b. If you want to be with me, no romance without finance." There's pressure that a man feels to be the breadwinner. Yes, even today with all of the progress that we've made, I've always felt the pressure that if I were not out there making things happen financially than I'm not fulfilling my role as the man of the family. Today, you have many women who make more money than their partners, but there's an internal struggle that I've always gone through when it comes to providing for my family. It was a way that I gained an identity. While I accepted this job with the incentive of making money, I learned quickly that

60

making money shouldn't motivate me to accept a job. Let's just say I see how more money doesn't equal happiness.

After my first month in my new and "exciting career," I knew that I was in the wrong place. I recall looking into the cubicle of a co-worker. I'm not sure of his age. While watching him, I wondered about how long he had worked there? He looked out-of-shape. He appeared to be unhappy. I kept hearing him sigh and complain about the workload. His desk had candy wrappers, a big coffee mug, and a couple bags of potato chips. He was balding, overweight, and looked grumpy. I thought to myself, there's no way that I want to be him twenty or even thirty years from now. How do I escape? What steps do I need to take to change my life now before it's too late? Instead of making adjustments, I chose to stay in this career path and continue to pursue the all-mighty dollar. A major concern was about what people would think about my making an irrational decision of quitting a job in "Corporate America" before getting married. Once again, this is a self-inflicted wound. While I believe that I would get this type of feedback if I decided to follow my passion, I have to own the fact that I didn't act on my desire. While I was spending time chasing the dollar, there was a desire chasing me. What was chasing me was a desire that I had for more in my life. I believe it's the inner voice that God uses to speak to us at times. This inner voice kept speaking to me, but I wasn't listening. There's more out there for you. By not following my inner voice, I was setting myself up for pain and disappointment.

My parents always taught me to be involved in my community to make a difference. So, I began helping a church, in my community, with its weekly activities and Sunday morning classes. This was something that I was raised to do. On

Tuesday, August 22, 1995, the pastor was praying over people, praying for encouragement, praying for the sick, and praying for people in need. Waiting for the service to end, I was sitting in the back of the church. I was looking at my watch and then all of a sudden, the pastor stopped the service and music. He pointed to the back of the church and said, "Stand up." I looked around and thought to myself, who, me? He said, "Yes, you, stand up!" He barely knew me; we only had one or two conversations since I had started going there. He told me about why God had moved me to a new city. God wanted to get me away from my protective environment in order to allow me to develop in the man that God wanted me to be. He told me that God wanted me to one day pastor a church. This was both shocking and exciting to me at the same time. It was shocking because how can this man that I had only spoken to a few times have any clue of things that I was dealing with in my heart? It was exciting because I was amazed that it felt as though God was talking directly to me. Earlier in this story, I mentioned that I had a tug in my heart. *This was the tug.* I knew somehow that I would become a pastor. I didn't know how it would look? People work as pastors in many ways. At this time, I thought that it was to pastor a church, so in my heart I was happy to hear that someone else had seen this in me. After the pastor finished speaking to me during the service, I just sat down with a startled look on my face. From that day, people kept calling me pastor. I didn't really know how to respond to that. While it was exciting to hear that God chose me to do something incredible for him. It was scary, and I wasn't sure if I really wanted to do become a pastor. I watched how people stepped out to trust God, and it looked as though life was working out for them. This brought up the memory of watching a friend of mine in while I was in college. He came to me and said that God had told him to leave the college we were attending and transfer to a seminary. I thought to myself, "He must be a nut, I mean who does that?" Well, he must have been nuts because that's exactly what he did. I saw another friend give up a great job offer to further his education because he believed that God had something for him to finish. As I began to develop a closer relationship with my pastor, I began to see something that many people don't get to see, his pain. He witnessed people close to him take advantage of his kindness. You may say well that happens to everyone, what makes the pain of a pastor so much different? A God appointed pastor is someone who genuinely cares for people. When the people they lead hurt, they hurt. There's a reliance on people close to them to be trusted confidants and friends. The pain that I witnessed came from hurt caused by those who were trusted by the pastor. On some occasions, the pastor was betrayed, criticized, and used. I did not want to subject myself or my family to abuse from ungrateful people. In addition, I witnessed pastors abusing their positions. I would see ministers peddling for offerings during services. Sometimes there would be not one, not two, not three, but up to four in a service. How many times can you ask the *same people* during the *same service* to give? I definitely believe that we have a responsibility to give, but what I saw was abuse and manipulation. Did I really want this? The church was full of people hurting and looking for hope. Each week, I saw many people leave disenchanted and discouraged. This was not the direction that I wanted to go in my life. This internal battle that I was having was leading me to a crossroads where I needed to make a decision. While I was sure that there were great things about being a pastor, these were the types of issues that stood out to me. I decided that I would answer God's calling to pastor, but I would do it on my terms. My terms were that I would impact the lives of people on an individual basis and not rely on their offerings to support me. I never wanted to be that guy who needed to depend on offerings for financial support.

Chapter 5 - Reflection Questions

1.   What element in your current

     situation fuels you?

2.   Do you have a "tug" in your

     heart? What is the "tug"?

3.   What are you doing about the

     "tug"?

Chapter 6
Walk the Path Meant for You

**"The journey of a thousand miles begins
with one step."**
-Lao Tzu
Never base a decision for your life on

what is happening in the lives of those

around you. I violated this principle when I

saw someone pursuing a career path, and I

thought to myself, that sounds like a good

direction for me. I remember the feeling

when I first heard a co-worker announce that she had been accepted to law school. I felt excitement for her, but there was also jealousy. That's what I always said that I would do when I was in college. The question was if I had planned on going to law school why didn't I do it after undergrad? Was there a sense of fear? Was there an excuse? What was the reason? The answer is I'm not sure. While looking into these next steps, I never truly considered the cost. Financial planners use a "risk tolerance tool" to help their clients evaluate their breaking points in investments. Evaluating our risk tolerance is another way of counting the costs when we decide to step out of our comfort zone. With every decision I make, I evaluate my risk tolerance. Then I decide whatever I think I can take *means I can take more.* The risk that we take in this life requires an element of faith. Sometimes we have to leap and see what the results will be.

I made the difficult and expensive decision to go to law school. To this day, I don't regret it, but I learned a lot about myself. Let me paint the picture for you. I was working full-time in a very demanding Corporate American job. I had only been married for two years; my wife and I had a one-year-old daughter and a son on the way.

74

I was going to law school at night. Can we say that I was taking on too much! Law school was an incredible struggle. I had a very difficult schedule of classes. The first day of class, the criminal law professor reviewed his policies. Eating in class was one of his pet peeves; I really didn't understand it. I mean you have working adults coming directly from their jobs to school at night without an opportunity to eat. Well, one day, I forgot about his rule of no eating in class. Rushing to school, I grabbed a Snickers candy bar on the way into his class. The entire class time, he kept calling on me to brief various cases. I thought that he must really like me, and I must be killing these cases. Then, it finally dawned on me; I was eating in his class. That night was merely a microcosm of my entire law school experience. The remaining months of law school were very challenging. I recall the stress and anxiety that I felt. My health wasn't very good. Because I didn't have time to exercise regularly and to eat correctly, I gained nearly twenty pounds. My full-time position wasn't very supportive of my decision to go to law school. My supervisor even mentioned to me that the company really didn't like lawyers. There were times when my department head would give me additional files and expect them to be handled in a timely manner. What I mean by timely is that we had two days to contact clients and ten days to resolve their issues. There was even a week when my manager had given the majority of my department time out of the office, and I was left there with two other people. I was the only experienced person. It happened to be a week that we were extremely busy. I ended up working nearly round the clock to ensure that I was able to keep up with my work and to attend my law classes. The mounting stress and expectations of my job, law school and family ultimately led me to an anxiety attack. On a Thursday morning

77

as I was preparing to leave the house for work, I felt a sharp and piercing pain in my chest. I couldn't breathe and thought that I was having a heart attack. I remember the fearful look on my wife's face. I thought to myself, is this how my life was going to end, working like a mad man, trying to finish a law degree. Would I miss out on having the opportunity to grow old with an incredible woman while raising two great kids. A few hours later, at the age of 27, I was in the hospital. After running a series of tests on me, the doctors determined that I had suffered a stress attack. For the first time in my life I truly began to reflect on the time

78

we have on the earth and the price of pursing purpose. According to Matthew 16:26, "what does it really mean if I gain the whole world and lose my soul?" Not trying to be preachy with this statement, but think about this. What exactly did I stand to lose? During this time in my life, I began to question what exactly is the "American Dream" and could it be a reality or is it just that, a dream? I needed to be reprogrammed. I needed to take an inventory of my life, circumstances, and the direction in which I was heading. The question was would I be willing to make the change or would I still continue trying my way?

One definition of insanity is doing things the same way but expecting different results. Let's just say that I've had some moments of insanity in my life. After my whole scare with the stress attack, I decided to leave law school and find balance in my life. While writing this, I'm laughing at myself because my decision to find balance in my life didn't last too long. I had an unsettled spirit about working the straight nine to five in Corporate America while receiving my $700 raise annually. Yeah!

I decided to throw my hat into the very lucrative real estate market of the 1990s. People were buying homes with no money down. Home values were good. You could bank on the fact that everyone needed a place to stay. Why shouldn't I be the one to help him or her find their ideal home? My ultimate plan for financial success and achieving the "American Dream" was to build my real estate empire. Can you blame me? Most millionaires and billionaires held some form of real estate in their portfolios. As I started down the same path again, you know the path in pursuit of the American Dream, I decided that it was time to diversify my portfolio. I obtained my real estate license, and I purchased my first rental property. This was it! I was beginning to build my empire. One problem is that the empire needed a very sound foundation. A long time ago, actor Tom Hanks stared in a movie entitled, *The Money Pit*. This movie had some memorable moments; it was the story of a newly married couple that purchased their dream home that needed a little work. In the movie, the home ended up costing them a ton of money and stress. The floors were coming apart. The roof caved in. Well, this describes our first rental property. I remember the closing day; it felt incredible to have my first investment property. Then we got the keys. Entering the house, I thought to myself, we have a lot of work to do. We began working hard - pulling carpet, tearing out old floors, and cleaning up the front of the house. My mindset was to treat this home as if I were going to move into it.

What I learned quickly is that just because you feel a certain way about a home doesn't mean that everyone else will. I also learned how well-mannered some people will act when they are interested in something that you have to offer. What I mean by this is that the tenants that we interviewed for our property put their best foot forward, but in reality, it was a facade. They wanted a nice home but didn't appreciate it because they didn't have any "skin in the game". There was no investment in maintaining the property. Let's just say that if Hollywood is looking for good actors, the casting directors should contact property owners to get a list of their tenants. There are a few Academy Award winners on the list. After placing an ad in the paper for renting out the home, we received a number of calls for the property. My wife scheduled an open house. Now the fun began. The first tenant who showed up was interesting. Let's call her Ms. Parker.

After filling out the application, we spoke with her. We asked about her employment and who would be living with her. There was a gentleman with her. I asked who was he? She replied, "This is my brother. He was just helping me look for a place to move." She also told me that she had a job. I decided that I would give her the benefit of the doubt and take her at her word. We allowed her to move into the newly rented house.

One of the responsibilities of a property owner is to conduct regular inspections of the property to ensure that property is in good shape. Well, during my first visit, guess who was in the living room watching the television at 1:30 in the afternoon? It was Ms. Parker's "brother." The house wasn't clean, and there were people all over the place. I thought to myself, "This was a horrible decision." What made it even worse is that it's not easy to evict someone from a property. In other words, I was stuck with this tenant for a year unless she stopped paying the rent. Eventually, this tenant moved out at the end of her lease. The aftermath of her residency was a disaster. We were left with a property that was in desperate need of repair. To top it off, she didn't give us notice that she had left the property. As a result, the home was vandalized. I discovered a property that had been completely gutted. I mean every window had been broken and the aluminum siding around it was taken. The ductwork was gone; they even took the downspouts and plumbing fixtures. It was a total nightmare! While I was thankful that I had insurance, it was one of the worst feelings in the world. This was a dream that I had to begin my real estate empire. What was I doing wrong? I must admit that I was thankful for that insurance company who referenced themselves as the good neighbor because the neighbors near the property became see no evil, speak no evil, and hear no evil. Fortunately, the repairs were completed to the property, and we were able to sell it. Talk about relief. I must admit at the time becoming a real estate tycoon seemed like a really good idea, but I quickly learned that wasn't cut out for that type of business.

Did I previously mention that I obtained my real estate license? Well, that was part of my master plan in developing my real estate empire. While working at my full-time corporate job during the day, I was working on building my real estate brand in the evenings. I've never been afraid of working hard. However, there is a difference in working hard and working smart. I had to make cold calls. This was the toughest part of the process until I came across a couple that said they were looking to purchase a home. I was excited; this could be my first sale of many. I scheduled to meet with them and reviewed their current situation. It looked as though things were in order and we could go forth. After taking them to a mortgage broker, they were pre-approved to purchase a home. I didn't want to break one of the cardinal rules of real estate and that was to take prospects around without getting them pre-approved. Then we began to go down the stressful path of trying to find the home for them. Let me be the first to say that I wanted to be an understanding and patient realtor. We went from house to house for nearly a month. After visiting twenty homes, they couldn't find anything to their liking. They were not being realistic. Being approved for $75,000 but having a $250,000 desire was not going to work. After seeing a number of homes, I decided to have a heart-to-heart conversation with them. They were not very receptive. According to the client, I wasn't finding the right homes for them. You know the saying, "The customer is always right." Well, that person didn't have this customer.

90

Eventually, we decided to end our business relationship. That was only the beginning of my frustrations as a realtor. Over the next few months I went on to meet with prospects and show them around. I even listed a few homes. After nearly a year, I had dealt with several unrealistic clients and had seen seven deals fall through. I never had an opportunity to sell a house; I decided that this might not be the path for me. Some may question me and say that I didn't hang in there long enough, but I would be quick to tell them that's not for them to decide. When they have spent some time in my shoes, then come and talk to me.

Life can be both exciting and scary at the same time. Some of you who are reading this may remember the Milton Bradley Company board game, "The Game of Life." You essentially have to progress through the game without making critical mistakes that can ruin your family's future. For example, a player can make a bad investment or having kids when you're not financially stable. It's a game that can help people from ages nine and up learn what it means to have the American Dream. That game presents life as a given roadmap that we all must follow to live a successful life. *It's a lie.*

92

There isn't a template that exists where everyone achieves success and happiness.

Next, I decided that I would venture into the "lucrative" world of insurance sales and open my own insurance agency. Finally, my opportunity had come. The office was located in a suburb of Cleveland, Ohio. My name was on the office building sign, "R.D. Collins Insurance Agency Inc." Even though, I didn't reap the monetary benefits of running my own business during this time, I did see how important I was to my wife and children! I would drive up to the office every day and I would see my name on the sign. It made me feel good as if I had arrived. Running an insurance agency wasn't my dream, it was the option that I finally had. I was able to provide financially for my family. You know like when you're watching those movies when they show the person who has the big corner office. They look successful, you know, as though they have made it. I had my staff of three people, and even my family was involved. My wife supported the business as the office manager. My daily schedule was under my control. Anytime, my family needed me to be available, I was there. I started to see what it was that I enjoyed about running my business. What I really liked was that ability to decide what happens to me on my own terms. While this time was one of the most difficult in my life financially, it was one of the most beneficial for me. I was able to coach my son and daughter in their respective sports. The look on those faces when I would show up made it all worth it. The highlight of my day was to pick them up from school. Yes, their father would pick them up for school and see them off each day. I am still reaping the benefits of this in my relationship with them. I was able to be a real father. A real father is there for his children, and yes, should be there to pick up his children from school. Don't believe what's depicted in society when you see the minivan pull up to school, and it's always the mom there to pick them up. There's a special bond when kids look up and see their father waiting on them after school. I can say this with all confidence that I had gained a good understanding of what my role was in my family and how important I was to the growth and development of my children. Ultimately, I believed that I mattered as a father and a husband.

Chapter 6 - Reflection Questions

1. What's your definition of the American Dream?

2. What does success look like for you?

Chapter 7
Shattered

"It can take years to mold a dream. It takes only a fraction of a second for it to be shattered" -Mary E. Patterson

It is dangerous to take failures too personally or seriously. A few years ago, I suffered one of the worst failures of my life. I decided to step away from a very comfortable job to venture into an opportunity that my wife and I truly believed that God was calling us to do. Feeling a calling to leave my job to create a new ministry, we decided to start a church. Not a church similar to where we were attending, but a church that would look so different that it would make people curious, welcomed and want to get to know God better. This was a difficult task because I had always attended or been a part of a church where mostly everyone was from the same ethnicity. We worshipped the same, we prayed the same, and even the preaching was similar. I believed in my heart of hearts that God wanted to do something new in my life and the lives of those who would join us on this journey. In order to do something different, I had to be different in my approach. As a result, I had to be willing to step out of my comfort zone and take a risk that others would understand and be able to see what I was seeing. The biggest risk was leading my family out to uncharted waters.

It started with my making a decision to let my current pastor who was also my employer know that I was leaving to do something that God had placed on my heart to do. This was hard because I held a lot of respect for him and never wanted to hurt him. Plus, there's a very different dynamic when a person works for a church and they also attend the same church. It was hard for this decision to not be taken personally. I also had a responsibility to God first and my family. In addition, I had to be true to myself.

How did God want this church to look? Anybody ever struggle with thoughts like this? I can raise both hands and feet. What I was really trying to figure out is what was going to be the vision of this church? What I learned during this time is that even though I had the vision, it still wasn't completely clear. I needed time to clear my head and to change my approach from what I had seen most of my life. Time was of the essence because I was paid a salary to plant a new church. As a result, my fundraising dollars were affected by how long it would take to start the new church. One of the biggest reasons why I struggled in this effort is that I didn't have the time needed. I continued to work on starting this church within a short time period while feeling pressured.

Another important principle, pressure will reveal what's inside of you. Just like when a tire gets a hole in it, all the pressure comes out. This is when I began to feel, but was it too late. Was I in too deep? That's crazy to say when talking about doing something for God, but I want to be honest.

I began to feel as though there was no other way out. I had already left my previous job. I was receiving a salary. There was a deadline. My family was counting on me. God was counting on me!

As a result of this self-inflicted pressure, the vision of the church struggled. I attended some leadership trainings and had meetings with other leaders who were leading churches. The trainings were meant to assist me in developing a vision for the ministry. This was difficult for me because they couldn't speak for me, think for me, and hear God for me. I should have been listening when I heard one of the leaders say to me that they didn't know what I was about. It wasn't a personal attack on me; it was an honest assessment at the time. If anything, I should have told him you're right.

I didn't even know how I should be approaching this. I didn't have time because I was being paid a salary, and I had a date to have the church opened. I previously mentioned that I had to raise funds for the church operations. In essence, raising funds involves sharing the vision with others and soliciting their financial support. I had to solicit financial help from associates, businesses, and other churches. This was truly the hardest part of starting the ministry. People will talk to you just about anything except their money. This is where the pain of the process began to happen. Other pastors told me that what I was trying to do was hard, but good luck. Instead of saying, "We can't support you financially right now, but maybe there's another way we can help." the response was "Good luck." Then I had to reach out to friends and family. This is where you think to yourself, "I know these people got my back." I thought that if anyone would understand my heart it would be people that I called friends and family.

Ironically, this is where I felt one of the biggest betrayals ever. People committed various amounts of financial support and very little came in. It began to feel as though what I was doing didn't matter. It was gut wrenching. Just imagine - you work hard to build a business. Spend all of your retirement to build the business. When opening day comes, no one is there.

I focused on the disappointment so much that it began to hurt my effectiveness in leading this new ministry. It manifested itself in the way I would prepare to preach on Sundays. I was struggling and really didn't let anyone in, not even my wife and children. *This was a deep hurt. I felt so alone.* It felt as though I was locked in a room and the walls, ceiling, and floor were caving in on me. The pressure was mounting to grow numerically as a church and financially through fund raising. I knew that the church couldn't survive on the resources that were coming in every Sunday. At times, anxious feelings would consume me. I was leading while bleeding. It was nice to have new people come around, but we were small in number and didn't have the resources that were expected of me by the organization that hired me. Mentors that I had in the past completely separated from me. Many of you reading this can relate to this situation right now. I hear it often that when you step out to do something different that you will not see the support from those you would expect and you will get support from those you least expect. That's one of the biggest problems with man. Just because someone leaves to do something different doesn't mean that he or she does not want the people who have been such a big part of the lives to leave. I would argue that these people are needed even more. I allowed hurt to take over. The hurt had such a profound effect on me that the church didn't even last six months. As a result of not having the financial support, it looked as though we were not going to make it. The organization that hired me decided it was time to close the church. In other words, I wasn't hitting my sales numbers. What happens to a salesman who can't sell? He is fired.

Before I go any further, please know that there were a few great things that came out of the ministry. God placed His servants with us during the time the church was open. There was an amazing couple, Ernest and Sharon, who relocated to Cleveland and they were looking for a church. This church allowed Ernest to grow closer to God. Brian and Suzanna, a beautiful couple, supported us through every step of the journey. Bernie was amazing and served tirelessly. We had a great children's leader in Owen. Alex and his wife Mariah moved to Cleveland from Oklahoma to help us. Jon and Rita were amazing in their support and how they shared with us each week.

With the impending close of the church, I recall the feeling of failure and embarrassment! I felt as though I let my family down. Although, I never heard one word of disappointment from my family, I had decided that I was a failure. As a man, you want to be the hero for your family! I heard the voices in my head, "Loser. Failure. Enough is enough. You will never succeed!" These thoughts of loneliness and failure took me to a very dark place. For the first time in my life, I knew how real depression looked. I was allowing a failed project to define who I was. The depression that I had allowed to take over blocked out anything positive that someone would say to me. It was so bad, that I couldn't read and didn't want to know what God thought about me. At times when I would be alone with my thoughts, I would feel a heavy presence of something or someone sitting with me helping me to go deeper in my darkness. I had a feeling of being at the bottom of a pit with no way to climb out of it.

The weekend that we had to announce to the church that we were going to close was a very tough one. The night before our service, my wife was feeling pain in her leg. The pain was so severe that she couldn't put any pressure on her leg. After going to the hospital, we discovered that my wife had a blood clot in her leg. She stayed in the Intensive Care Unit for four days. *I couldn't handle one more thing.* Take note that I had not talked with anyone about how I was really feeling. I was holding it all in to protect my family; at least that was the lie I was telling myself. The next day came, and I announced to the group of people who were still worshipping with us that the church would be closing. I noticed the hurt on the faces of the people. Instead of trying to help them process the closing of the ministry, I sank even lower into my own feelings of failure. The emotional pain with which I was dealing was relentless. When you see the pot on the stove full of hot water boiling over - that's what was going on inside of me. After the blood clot began to heal, my wife came home. I wonder what's worse recovering from a physical ailment or an emotional one?

The feeling of being alone can create a sense of hopelessness. I need you to really take this seriously and recognize when someone close to you is struggling. You need to take inventory of the people in your life. Never let them feel alone. At times we can become so busy that we forget to take the time out to check in on loved ones. Just think, if each person would take some time to look in on someone, no one should ever feel alone.

I need you to pay close attention to this next section of the story. I want to let you inside a very personal part of my life. As a human and even more so as a man, it's hard to open up and make yourself vulnerable. I believe that it's important to share with others when there is hurt going on inside. Far too often, there are people who are smiling daily while dying. It's time to create a safe culture for everyone to be willing to be open and honest. No longer should we live in the fear of being vulnerable because of the concern of worrying what someone will think or say about us. I recall sharing my story with someone, and his or her reply to me was you were just weak at that time. What person wants to hear that he or she is weak? In reality, I was just broken. I was shattered on the inside and didn't know what steps were necessary to put me back together. After spending a few weeks struggling and trying to process all of the pain that I had been enduring inside, I had hit my limit. One day I was sitting in my home. My wife was at work. My son and daughter were at school. I remember the thoughts in my head. "Look at what your decision has done to your family." "You told all of those people what God wanted you to do." "You look like a fool." This was the first time that those thoughts returned to me about my childhood friend who took his own life. I actually understood how he felt so low. *It was that sense of failure.* The feeling that life wouldn't get better gave me the feeling of all the walls were closing in on me and eventually it was going to end. I felt an incredible darkness over me; it was as if someone else was in my home with me. Once again, I was alone in my thoughts. I was such an emotional wreck at that time. I felt a piercing feeling in my chest; I couldn't breathe. My heart was pounding. I began to sweat. Tears began to roll down my eyes. There were so many memories flashing through my mind. Although the sun was shining into my living room where I was sitting, it felt like the entire room had become dark. Then, I heard a voice in my head, "Go to the garage, start up your car, and die!" *Did I really want to die? I don't think so.* I loved my family and wanted to see my son and daughter grow up. I wanted to grow old with my wife. There still remained this thing called pride. I was struggling with the fact that my income had drastically declined. I was tired of struggling financially and just wanted to be over it. I said to myself, "You have life insurance; your family doesn't need a loser. They need the money!" "Go get in the car, turn it on, and just die!" I got up and grabbed the keys. I opened up the door and went into the garage. As soon as I put my hands on my car door I suddenly stopped. I heard, "Okay go ahead and do this, who is going to be the first person to find you?" "What are you teaching your son when things get tough as a man?" "Do you care about your daughter?" "Why would you leave such a wonderful and dedicated woman?" "Do you really think the money would solve this problem?" Tears began to come down my face. I dropped to my knees beside the car. I failed at something once again. I was angry with myself for not being able to go through with it. I couldn't go through with taking my life because there was someone who came to save me. *God was there.* During this battle in my mind, there was someone fighting for me. Through all the pain and disappointment, God was there.

At times in our lives we wonder if God really cares about us. Many people question where is God when a tragedy happens. This emotional struggle had caused me to question my faith. I wondered if God truly loved me or even cared about what I going through. *At that moment, I realized that God was always there for me watching.* He was waiting for me to acknowledge that I needed Him. God is a gentleman and doesn't force Himself into your life. God lets you know that He loves you. HE is willing to be in involved in your life if you are willing to invite Him into it.

True strength comes from being able to recognize when you need help. When my wife came in the house, I told her that I was broken and I needed help. It was one of the hardest things that I had to do. I had to admit that emotionally I wasn't well. For too long, we, as men, have been made to feel as though we are weak when we have revealed that we are hurting. What I learned during that moment is that I was stronger than I had ever been. Being open and honest

120

about how vulnerable I had become allowed my wife to see me. After my wife listened to me, she held me. It felt good for me to have an understanding woman who wouldn't judge me but let me know that she was with me at my most vulnerable moment in life. I believe at that I began the healing process. One of the first steps in healing is to admit that you're hurting. My wife gave me a safe place to admit that I was depressed and needed help. There was a feeling of guilt and shame to show my family how weak I had become. In reality, I was at my strongest moment of this test because I realized that I was broken and needed help.

In order to get through this difficult time in my life, I knew that I needed to see a therapist. Yes, I said it! I decided to get counseling. Unfortunately, for many years, some people in the black community did not recognize the need for professional therapists. I listen to the nationally syndicated talk show, "The Breakfast Club" on a regular basis. The host, "Charlemagne tha god" frequently talks about his issues and his commitment to meet with his therapist on a regular basis. I admire and respect that brother for being real, open, and honest. I believe there's an awakening happening in the black community where it is no longer taboo to get counseling to deal with mental and emotional issues. *Depression is a real.* *It's not something to just get over.* It doesn't mean that a person is weak. No one can tell another person about his or her hurt and how they should be processing it. The key is to recognize the hurt that leads to depression and acknowledge that help is needed.

Chapter 7 - Reflection Questions

1. What's your dream?

2. Have you counted evaluated the risk associated with fulfilling your dream?

3.   Who are your supporters and

      what role do they plan in your

      life?

4.   How would you define the word

      "depression?"

5.   Do you know where you can go

      for help?

*Where to go for assistance

USA – The Lifeline: 1-800-273-TALK (8255)
UK & Ireland – The Samaritans: 116-123
Canada – Crisis Services Canada: 1-833-456-4566
Australia – Lifeline: 13-11-14
New Zealand – Lifeline: 0800-543-345

Chapter 8
Mending the Broken Pieces

"Instead of saying, "I'm damaged, I'm broken, I have trust issues" say, "I'm healing, I'm rediscovering myself, I'm starting over." -Horacio Jones

I know that this is a book about purpose, but in discovering my purpose and making a decision to pursue it with undying conviction I went through several failures. Those failures unbeknownst to me were part of the process. I knew that I couldn't do it alone anymore. I needed an impartial party who could look at my life with an open and unbiased opinion. I decided that I needed to talk to a professional therapist. For the next six months following this incident, I met with a counselor who helped me walk through and unpack the layers that led to my depression. It was one of the best investments that I made in myself. I was holding in so much hurt and bitterness. I discovered that one of my most deeply rooted struggles was forgiveness. The first person that I had to forgive was myself. It's a pride thing. There's a feeling that failure, for a man, is not an option. There's a sense of competition that's so deeply embedded in us that it can make a subtle entrance into every area of our lives. For example, we try to keep up with the Joneses; compete against a family legacy, or struggle with "ghosts" that hold a stronghold on our lives. I'm highlighting all of these challenges because during the process of my counseling these issues began to surface. What I thought I should become since I was a young boy had been heavily influenced by society's standards that have been ingrained in my soul since I was a kid. So, while you're reading this right now, ask yourself, what's still driving me? What are the wrong influences and the so-called positive influences that have made you the person that you think you're supposed to be? I had to process all of the choices that I had made.

127

Ultimately, I realized that no matter the circumstances - I am responsible for my life and I need to own it. The most important thing we have to do when we experience disappointment is admitting that we're hurting and need help. It's the process of admitting that a man or woman or child can be hurt. My demonstrating the emotions that were inside of me did not make me less of a man. By being open with my emotions, I was being as courageous as I had ever been in my life. *There was a sense of freedom with transparency.* Putting on a facade that everything is okay is something we have been conditioned to do. We like everyone to

128

see us as without problems, concerns or worries. The outside looks as though all is well. While on the inside we're broken, beaten, bruised, and bleeding.

I don't ever want someone to experience feeling alone; this is an awful feeling. The sad fact is that today, there are still a number of people who live in homes with family and friends, yet they're still struggling with feelings of inadequacy, feelings of being alone, and feelings of abandonment. I want you to know that help is available. *Love the person you see in the mirror every morning.* You must be able to look that person in the eye and deal with whatever challenges are present. Anything that we try to suppress will reveal itself in other destructive ways. In order to move forward in life, there must be a decision to look at everything that's going wrong and realize that you can't get through it alone. God didn't place you and me on this earth with seven billion people to live life alone. It was God's grace that rescued me. It was my family that rescued me. I realized that no matter what mistakes or failures happen that my presence is what my family wanted! Isn't that what we all really want?

We all want to feel that we are needed. It gives us a sense of purpose and a sense of belonging. Purpose is the driving force that gives us the energy to get up and step outside of our homes every day. When you hear the question, *what's your why*, it's really asking, what's your purpose? Without purpose, it's easy to give up. I want you to know that in your efforts to achieve success, know what success really means to you. Don't let anyone define success for you, but God! God defines purpose, based on how He has wired you. There's no one that knows each of us so intimately as God does. Jeremiah 1:5 says, "Before I formed you in the womb I knew you, before you were born I set you apart; I appointed you as a prophet to the nations."

In order to move forward, there were several steps that I had to take to regain emotional control over my life. There's a scripture in the Bible, Philippians 2:3 says, "Let nothing be done through strife or vainglory, but in lowliness of mind each counting other better than himself." One thing that truly led to my healing was when I started to get outside of my feelings and I began to realize that there were people in more difficult situations than I was. I was challenged each day to find someone who needed my help. *Take time out each day and see how you can help someone.* I have found that when we are intentional about looking for the needs of someone else that we will definitely find a need. Taking time to help someone in need took my focus off of my circumstances. There was one person in particular who was in need. Struggling at home and at school, he was a young man who had a lot of anger inside. He had an older brother who was always in trouble. One time he had challenged me to a fight because I wouldn't allow him to disrespect a few teenage girls. He was an angry young man who saw in me the disappointment that

133

he felt in his father. I realized that in order to reach this young man, I would have to understand what was going on in his world. As a result, I took a different approach to connect with him. I heard that he was very competitive and out of all the things he liked to do was to play chess. When I would see him, I would invite him to play me in chess. His eyes would be blood shot red from all the marijuana he was smoking, but he was cognizant enough to play me in chess. During those times, I would come up with ways to talk to him and discover what was going on in his world. What he saw in me was something that he really didn't see in adults, especially men. The young man saw that I genuinely cared about him and what was going on in his life. We went on to develop a real friendship. I believe he began to respect me because he saw that I was concerned about him and respected him. Each day, I went out of my way to find him and make sure that we played chess and talked. I saw firsthand that people don't care how much you know and until they know how much you care. *That's my challenge to you.* Don't just show up to help someone as though you're some kind of superhero who has arrived to save the day. In reality, you're there to learn and grow to understand

135

what it really means to serve mankind. Yes, I said serve. Real transformation takes place in someone's life through the vehicle of service.

Secondly, I began to look at my life each day and to find reasons to be grateful for the gift of life. Life-speaking affirmations were placed around the house. I wouldn't allow any negativity in my life. As a result, I started to look at my wife, my son, and my daughter in a different way. I cherished Falanda, my beautiful wife, who had stood by my side through so many ups and downs and never put me down as a man. I know there were some times in her mind when she was thinking this dude is making all of these moves, can he just decide on one and stick to it. She may have thought it, but she never said it to me. I have a daughter and a son who have grown into incredible young adults.

Thirdly, I finally decided that I loved me for who I was, and I believed in the person that I saw in the mirror on a daily basis. I used to think there was a problem with loving myself. I mean who wants to be that guy who is conceited and selfish. In order to avoid that mindset, I was at the other extreme. I would be self-deprecating. In essence, I would use speech to keep me lowly. That was the worst idea ever. By having that mind-set, I was saying that God had made mistakes with me. Being stuck with this type of thinking kept me from moving forward to receive what God had for me. I had to see that if I didn't see my value and believe in my worth that no one else would see it either. I want to encourage you right now to know that no matter what you've done, where you come from, or what you have done, you still have value! Nobody can put a value on you.

In my constant search for purpose, my wife and I had the opportunity to travel to Monrovia, Liberia, on a service trip. I was so excited and nervous about this trip for so many reasons. For one, it would be our first time traveling to the Motherland! To be a person of African descent, it's always been important for me to have an idea of my ancestry. I recall being in school and hearing students talk about their family trees and being very clear on where their family originated. The time had come for the flight to Monrovia. This would be the longest flight of my life, fourteen hours; I was constantly waking up to see if we were almost there. There was an excitement and anticipation like a child on Christmas Eve who can't sleep at night. Then, finally our plane landed in Monrovia, Liberia. I was so excited. I saw this as an opportunity to change lives. The host family that picked us up was very warm and excited to see us. I told one of the members of the host family that I couldn't wait to get there. I had been praying for them and for what God wanted to do. Then, suddenly the wife said in her beautiful African accent, "No, my brother, you see we have been praying for you. Because your country is very far from God, you worship Him for what He gives you. We worship Him only for who He is!" Let's say I was stumped. I mean what do you say to something like that. It gave me the biggest lump in my throat. From that moment, I knew that this time was more about what God wanted to do in me than what I wanted to do for God. Over the next few weeks, my perspective on life took on new meaning. Melton was a young man who was always around us during our time in Africa. I watched as he always demonstrated love and compassion for his people. He made himself readily available for anything that we needed. There was a sense of pride that he had in his homeland. We would have talks daily. He had such a joyful demeanor. I noticed that Melton did not have many personal belongings. He didn't have a lot of clothes; he didn't have

141

any jewelry. He didn't define himself by what he had. He found a reason to be grateful every single day in spite of his circumstances. He even knew how to have fun. This was surprising to me because I always believed that poverty equated to depression and sadness. One day, I was in need of a haircut. Take note, there was only limited electricity and running water. So, going into a local barbershop would present an interesting experience. Melton and another friend, Fred, took me to a barber. The barber invited me to sit in the chair. As I was getting into the chair, I saw the barber reach for a pack of razor blades. I had to maintain my composure because I didn't want to offend him in anyway. I closed my eyes and there was no sound from a barber's clippers. I began to feel the razor blade as he used the razor blade to cut my hair. I was extremely nervous, but for some reason I trusted someone that I didn't know to cut my hair in a way that I had never experienced. In a way, there was a sense of confidence in this barber. After getting my hair cut, it was time to head back to our residence. Well, we decided to continue our adventure and take a taxi back. This had to be one of the funniest and scariest experience I ever had. We hailed a taxi and when he pulls up the car is full. Take note, this car is a small hatchback. I couldn't tell what type, I just knew that it was very small! Maybe there was enough room for four people. In addition, it was a two-door car. A passenger opened the door; each seat was already taken. So, one passenger slid over and motioned for the three of us to get in. I looked at Melton and Fred! We all squeezed in the small vehicle! When in Rome, you do as the Romans do. I guess when in Liberia, you do as the Liberians do. There were seven of us jammed into a small four-passenger car! The thoughts that went through my mind! What if we get into an accident? What if the air conditioning stops working? What if someone passes gas!!! You're talking about facing fears and being willing to grow and understand another culture. This three-mile ride felt like a thirty-mile ride. Let's just say I wasn't disappointed when this trip ended. When we got out of the car, Fred and I had a good laugh. I never expected to have such a joyous experience while venturing out into the community.

Then came two of the most impactful moments for me during this time. First, my wife had an opportunity to teach a class at the school. I observed a classroom filled with over forty high school students. The students sat quietly at their desks with the hands folded and actually listened to my wife. They raised their hands to ask a question; no one was talking out of turn. There was a level of respect for education that puts our schools to shame. The people valued the opportunity to sit in a classroom and learn. Learning was not a task of frustration but a daily opportunity to grow. What makes a people appreciate something like education to this degree? After I spent time contemplating what I witnessed, I had to come to the conclusion that when you've experienced a loss of something that you

146

once had and the opportunity comes back, you have a greater appreciation for what that opportunity brings. The people of Liberia had been through a civil war that completely destroyed their infrastructure. Families were torn apart. Death was everywhere. At the time, the average life span of someone in Liberia was into the late thirties to early forties. As a result of the devastation and horror that was witnessed by the people, it appeared to me that each day was truly seen as a gift and that life was precious. After my time in Africa, I believe this to be true. At times, I wonder if our nation is heading for some type of major event that we help bring us up to where we should be?

147

Chapter 8 - Reflection Questions

1. In what ways are you looking out for the needs of others?

2. For what things are you grateful?

3. How do you define comfort?

4. Now, what would it take for you to leave that comfort?

Chapter 9
A Shattering Surprise

"God made you a masterpiece, stop treating yourself like a shattered piece."
-TemitOpe Ibrahim

What I have learned is that God has a way of bringing relationships back to you when you least expect it. I received a job offer to relocate to Los Angeles, California. Los Angeles is where I wanted to be. You remember I pastored a church, which meant that I was a licensed minister. Well, I was minding my own business at work when someone yelled out my name; it was someone who had attended the church that I had pastored. He was excited to see me, and he told me that he was getting married. I was happy for him and told him congrats. He told me that he was hoping to run into me because he wanted me to perform the wedding. I'm thinking to myself how funny life is because I hadn't seen this guy in over a year. It really caught me off guard because why me? He wanted me to be a part of his marriage because of the impact that I made on his life. Hearing him say how I influenced his life helped me to realize that we have more influence in the lives of people than we realize. Furthermore, it reminded me that my six months as a pastor was not in vain. I decided that I would be honored to perform his wedding. A few months later came the time for the wedding. While attending the rehearsal dinner, I had the opportunity to meet his family. During our time, I shared with them the vision I had for my family to relocate to Los Angeles, California. I talked about the experiences in life that brought us to the desire to relocate. What I didn't know is how closely the father of the groom was listening to me. *Here's another nugget. Always be clear on your vision before sharing it because you never know who is listening and can help your vision come to pass.* We had a great time that weekend, and I performed their wedding ceremony. A few weeks passed then I received a call from the groom's father. He asked me if I could stop by his office one day. The next day I dropped by his office. While waiting in his conference room, he comes in and says I have a job offer for you. I had a very puzzled look on my face. Who just offers a job to someone without a resume or at least a job application? I had many questions. What are the details of this job, where is it, and how much does it pay? He tells me that the job is in Los Angeles. Now, I'm thinking what is going on? I was looking for this type of offer! While this was exciting, I knew that I had to get more answers. Needing to do my due diligence, I didn't immediately accept the job. While researching the offer and the person offering me the job, my wife and I decided that we would accept the employment opportunity. This was the beginning of the next chapter of our lives, an exciting and challenging time. Our family was already going through a series of changes and now we're looking to moving across the country. This was my son's senior year and our daughter was a freshman in college. My wife didn't have a job in California. There were feelings of hesitation and concern over what our family was getting ready to go through and would this be the right thing to do. I took the time to speak with my family to make sure we were in agreement with this major decision. As a father, I was concerned also because I have always been involved in every aspect of my family. By accepting this job, I wasn't going to be present on a daily basis as I had been. This brought up thoughts of anxiety. I'm very close with my family and never wanted to miss any important moment in their lives. Then there's the thought of not seeing my wife every day. This was not an easy decision. Is pursuing a dream worth sacrificing everything you know? When an opportunity is presented, it must be vetted.

When an opportunity is presented, prayers must be said. When an opportunity is presented, God's directions must be followed. Asking God if this is path for me doesn't mean that there's a lack of trust in God or yourself. There are questions that must be addressed and commitments made. We made a decision that we were going to relocate our family, and I would start the process by accepting this job. This took incredible faith because we didn't have a place to stay, my wife didn't have a job, and we were moving across country while our two young adults would be in college. We were agreeing that as a husband and wife we

155

wouldn't see each other on a daily basis.

This was a true test of our marriage. Know that when you are in pursuit of a dream and purpose, you must have people in your life who agree with you. You need the closest people in your life to stand with you. You need to make sure that you have the right people on the bus with you. What I mean by the right people is that there's a level of support that's needed. It's very difficult to travel a road when people who are traveling with you want to go in a different direction.

After arriving in Los Angeles to begin my new job, I show up at the office to meet my employer's business partner. I ring the office doorbell and one of the associates comes to the door. I let him know who I am and that I had just arrived in town from Cleveland to launch the program. To my surprise, I wasn't allowed to enter the office and was told that the business partner wasn't aware of my arrival on that day. I'm not sure how anyone else would handle this, but I recall feeling my heart beating fast and I began to sweat. I was thinking to myself, I left a job for this job and drove over 2,000 miles across the country to begin this job and the first day I learn that things are not in place as I was told! Panic begin to set in. What should I do? The first thing I did was to call my employer, and I explained to him what happened. He didn't seem to be concerned and told me that he would follow up with his business partner. We talked about how we would address the situation. This gave me some comfort, not much, but at least I felt as though I wasn't alone. I was confident that I was not deceived into taking a job that really didn't exist. However, for me, the handwriting was on the wall. This position was in trouble, and I knew that I needed to figure something else out. I recall hearing that you should never leave your life in the hands of another man because that man is more concerned about his agenda than your well-being. I admit that at this time I began to start looking at this situation in preparation of self-preservation. There was a time when I would have been concerned with my employer's position.

Now, I realized that the person who offered me the position had a business in another city and he had achieved success. If this program was unsuccessful, he would still have his company and other projects, but I would be the one who would need a place to work. Funny thing about this situation, I started writing this book during that time. I wanted to be able to tell my story and help someone to navigate all the ups and downs we experience in this life.

On my ninth day in Los Angeles, while working on the launch of the new program, I had an accident. I'm driving on the freeway and the traffic is stop and go. Suddenly, the car in front of me stopped. I felt a push in my back and a loud noise. Someone had just rear-ended me and pushed me into another vehicle! Are you kidding me! It was one of the most frustrating things for me. I recall waiting by my car for the police to show up and the person who hit me came up to me and said, "It doesn't look that bad, maybe it can be fixed?" You should have seen the look that I gave him. He realized that it was best for him to return to his car and wait. Upon the police officer's arrival, the office asks me, "Do you think you can drive it home?" I wanted to show respect to the officer, but he was clearly joking with me trying to lift my spirits. After my car is towed, I have to wait at a restaurant for my first ride in an Uber. What made me laugh and feel as though everything would be okay was a notification that my Uber was close to me and it said, "Arriving Now 3:48 P.M. JESUS is arriving now in a Ford Fusion." Now we all know that Jesus doesn't drive an Uber, but there was a man named Jesus pronounced (hay-Soos) who was sent to pick me up. I laughed so hard because I knew the name wasn't what I thought, but it gave me some assurance that no matter what, I wasn't alone. I felt God's telling me that through the fire, I am with you; I will show up at the right moment in your life. This message was so significant because of its timing. I had been experiencing a lot of issues in the move, and I was rapidly approaching a breaking point. After being in the car accident, I felt that discouragement was moving in and setting up a permanent spot in my heart. Yet, I must say that it was amazing that through a stressful event, the accident that totaled my car, I was able to see purpose and promise.

I presently live in Los Angeles, California. Here we have wildfires. Fire is an element that refines and purifies. While they can be devastating, I've found that there is a purpose for them also. According to California Wildlife Experts, a wildfire has benefits to the ecosystem. Established trees have to compete with undergrowth for nutrients and space. Fire clears the weaker trees and debris and returns health to the forest. Here are a few other benefits of a wildfire: 1. Forest fires help prevent disease. 2. They provide nutrients for new

163

generations of growth. 3. It refreshes habitat zones. Ultimately, a forest fire clears thick growth so sunlight can reach the forest floor and encourage growth of native species. Basically, what I'm saying is that although something dies from the fire, it prepares the way for something new to come forward. This is what I was seeing in the pressure and stress that were coming my way. The heat that I was feeling was burning things out of me that were preventing from growing and moving forward. So, I must credit the loss of a job, the failure of a business and losing friends to the one hundred and eighty degree change I've made in my life.

I had to come to the conclusion that everything that I've experienced both good and bad has been the result of my choices. Did other people play a role? Yes, they did. Ultimately, I had to realize that I am responsible for my life. Do I believe that God plays a role in my life? Yes, I do. What I have learned about my walk with God is that He is a gentleman. He won't force His will on me. As I look in the mirror each day, I know that the person that I see can be my greatest ally or my greatest enemy. What I'm saying is that I had to forgive. I had to forgive God, yes, I said I had to forgive God, at one point through my journey; I blamed God for my circumstances, failures, and pain. I had to forgive each person that I reached out to who didn't respond. I had to forgive the person that I look at in the mirror. I learned that harboring hard feelings and not forgiving others led to my depression. It led to my feelings of inadequacy. Having an unforgiving heart was eating me alive at the core of my being. Forgiving others was the most liberating feeling that I had in years.

The past few years, my family has gone through the process of relocating from Ohio to California. This has been a challenging process with hurdles at every corner. We decided that we would no longer allow the hurdles to stop us. Life will always present challenges. I am determined to no longer allow exterior circumstances to dictate what I believe about who I am and what I can accomplish.

I'm glad to say that my story is still being written, just like many of you reading this book! The difference is that some are writing their stories with purpose. They know where there are going; they have goals that they are pursuing. For others, there is still a story, but the difference is they may not know their purpose. We are constantly searching for purpose and to be relevant. I think we learn what God wants and how our purpose looks when we're not afraid to step out and do something different. I'm a believer that purpose isn't found in the everyday comfort of our lives. Purpose is found when a person has a burning desire, some people call it passion, to see something accomplished. It's a desire inside that even if a person tries to get it to go away - it may subside for a moment, but it will bubble back up in the person.

Each disappointment that I've experienced has guided me to this point in my life. The young child who dreamed of what it would be like to be an actor is living his dream. I am now an actor, author, speaker, and mentor living in Los Angeles, California. This is an amazing journey. I am personally witnessing doors being opened by showing up and trusting God to provide the opportunities at the right time. I have been connected with influential decision makers in Hollywood and my career is encouraging others to start their own journey.

I have to say that I live life one mile at a time! What I mean is that I am intentional about being present. Present during every moment of my life. Being present doesn't mean that I'm not concerned about tomorrow. It means that I understand that each minute of life is a gift and I don't take that lightly. As I mentioned at the beginning of this book, the average human lives 28,000 days. This equates to 76.71 years, 40,320,000 minutes, 672,000 hours. While this time may seem like a lot, there's another important fact associated with the 28,000 days. The average human sleeps away 1/3 of this time. In essence 25 years of our life

170

is slept away. As a result, we spend 50 years living. My question for you to ponder as you read this book is what have you done with yours lately, and what will you do with the ones you have left? We all have purpose. We have goals. We have plans. Focus on the time that's right in front of you.

To the reader of this book, right now you should take the time to thank those in your life who sacrificed for you. No matter what their faults are they gave their best for you! Never forget from where you have come. Every experience that you have in life will trace back to your upbringing. Wherever you're from, whoever raised you is a part of who you are today, good and bad. Be bold in the person that you are and never let anyone take this away from you!

I want to encourage you to not be afraid to venture out of your comfort zone. The thing that you want to do, but fear doing, is most likely what you should be pursuing. For example, are you ready to start that business that you keep putting on the backburner? Do you want to travel to another country? Are you ready to leave your nine to five job, but afraid of the unknown? *This life we live is short.* Psalm 103:15-16 says, "The days of man are like grass. He grows like a flower of the field.

When the wind blows over it, it is gone."
You want to make your time count! At the
present moment of writing this book, I'm
leading my family into a new adventure.
I'm showing my son and daughter to not be
afraid to trust God. We are trusting God for
greater. One thing that I've learned in my
journey that the greater we achieve is not for
us, but for people to see God working
through our lives. It's for the world to see
how much He loves us and truly desires the
best life for us.

One of the biggest struggles for a young
person is determining what path he or she is

meant to follow. It's difficult to know which choice is the right choice. For example, what school to attend and what major to pursue can lead to both the most frustrating and exciting things in life. As a matter of fact, my wife and I are having countless discussions right now with our two young adults on what they desire to do. We have invested an incredible amount of time working with our son and daughter to help them to understand what it looks like to have a plan for their lives. Since they were young, we have instructed our son and daughter that we wanted them to be happy with their chosen careers. We've always desired for them to trust God for direction in their lives. The best way to show them was to live boldly and have faith in God and trust Him. As a result, we are giving them a living example of what it means to live a life without limits. It is our prayer that as they see our faith in action, they will be compelled to build their own relationship with God and trust God and know how to navigate the shattering moments in their lives.

Whatever God has placed in you is for a purpose! You may not fully understand it at the time, but during the journey you can focus on impacting each life that you

175

encounter. I must say that I am at peace with my journey! Everything that I've experienced in my life has led me to where I am today. I'm living life without limits! I'm not afraid because I know who holds me and has plans for me. One of my favorite passages in the Bible is Jeremiah 29:11. It says, "I know the thoughts I think towards you says the Lord, plans to not harm you, but to give you hope and a future!" No matter what life brings and it tries to hit hard, I know that my God puts a shield around me to withstand the blow. My race may be difficult, but this will help someone else's path be smoother! Understand that having some broken pieces in the journey makes the destination much sweeter. I can truly say that I love my life and the journey that I'm on. *Is it perfect?* Not at all, but I have decided to perfectly live, being present and allowing the pieces of my shattered journey to create a portrait that will last forever!

Chapter 9 - Reflection Questions

1. What is the biggest obstacle to pursuing your dreams?

2. What steps can you make in the next six months to position yourself to see one of your dreams happen?

3. Will your dreams help to improve the lives of other people? Why or why not?

Key Points to Live By

1. Count the cost of success.
2. Avoid permanent solutions for temporary problems.
3. Walk your own path.
4. Be intentional in looking out for someone's needs.
5. Show someone that you care before you try to help.
6. Love the person that you see in the mirror each day.
7. Always be clear on your vision before sharing it.
8. Pray and keep praying

Key Points to Remember

1. We want to matter.
2. Dreams indicate your wiring.
3. Most of our pain comes from self-inflicted wounds.
4. God has the best plan for your life.
5. Pray and keep praying.

Acknowledgments

I want to thank God from whom all my blessings flow for inspiring me to write this book and to share it with others. I want to thank my beautiful wife of twenty-three years, Falanda, who has stood by me and has inspired me. Get ready to reap the incredible blessings on our way! I want to thank my two beautiful children, Anointyd and Josiah, who are incredible blessings. I'm so grateful to have you as my children; my greatest prayer for you is that you develop a relationship with Jesus and for you to fully understand your purpose in Him. I am also grateful for my parents because they have been an awesome inspiration to me. To Mom and Dad, your countless sacrifices for your family have not gone unnoticed. You have raised me to love and lead my family. To my brothers, Mack and Sheldon, I am thankful for all the years that God has given us to walk together in this life. To Louis Farmer, I want to take a moment right now to say thank you for your boldness in connecting me with the perfect woman for me! I'm forever thankful for you making this step. To Sylvia Stewart-Lumpkin, thank you for being there for our family and for guiding me in writing this book. To the few good brothers who have been more than friends, thank you. You have shown me that the blessings of true friendship. To the countless others in my life who have made a significant impact, I want to thank you for every lesson that I've learned and the motivation to share my journey in this book. It is my prayer that this book will inspire you to share your stories with someone else. Stories inspire, stories motivate, and stories are real, so always remember your story matters to someone!

About the Author

Rodney Damon Collins is an actor, author, motivational speaker, and life coach. He holds a Bachelor of Arts Degree from Bowling Green State University. He also holds a Master of Religion (Leadership) and a Master of Divinity from Liberty University. He lives in Los Angeles, California, with his wife of twenty-three years and their two young adult kids. He can be seen on several television programs and has several motion picture projects coming up. As Rodney travels the country, he shares encouragement and hope. His mission is to infuse people with the motivation needed to live the life they were meant to live.

For bookings and speaking engagements contact: rodneydamoncollins@gmail.com or Instagram @rodneydamoncollins.

53311390R00114

Made in the USA
Lexington, KY
29 September 2019